Thi:

Mary Dyer
Friend of Freedom

by John Briggs

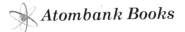

Atombank Books

Published by Atombank Books, Guilderland, NY

Edited by Albany Editing, Scotia, NY

Cover Illustration: *A Fair Puritan* by E. Percy Moran, 1897

Biography: Mary Dyer, Friend of Freedom by John Briggs. The life of civil rights and religious leader Mary Dyer (1611-1660). Colonial America.

ISBN: 978-0-9905160-0-2

To my great-grandmother, Esther Briggs, an ardent admirer of Mary Dyer, and to my son, John King Briggs, that he may someday admire her, too.

TABLE OF CONTENTS

MARY DYER, LOYAL FRIEND

Mary Dyer walked into church on March 22, 1638, ready for an argument. The people of Boston, Massachusetts, had turned against her best friend and teacher, <u>Anne Hutchinson</u>. Four months earlier, town leaders had banished Anne from her home; now they were banishing her from her church. Would Mary join her or beg the people to show mercy?

The problem for the people of Boston was simple. They belonged to the Puritan Church and did not like people who disagreed with them. Anne and Mary were both Puritans, but they didn't believe everything the Puritans did. The Puritans had very strict beliefs about God. They thought only ministers could teach the Bible and that people had to do good deeds if they wanted to get into heaven. Anne and Mary believed that anyone could speak to God and that people did not need to go to church to learn the Bible. Anne also taught that both men and women could be preachers, even though most Puritans believed only men should preach. Anne felt that faith in God and being a good person were more important than following the Puritan's laws.

Puritan leaders were among the most powerful people in Boston, and they worried that Anne's ideas would stop people from coming to church. The Puritans said people like Anne and Mary were breaking the law and called them "antinomians," which comes from a Greek word meaning "against the law." Puritan leaders urged Massachusetts Governor John Winthrop to arrest and banish all antinomians, so the governor charged them with **heresy**—the crime of disobeying religious teaching.

Mary Dyer was one of Anne's most ardent followers. She believed that women and ordinary people could teach the word of God. Even though Mary was twenty years younger than Anne, they were good friends. Now that friendship was being put to the test.

Anne had mocked one of the Puritan ministers, the Reverend John Wilson, saying he wasn't fit to preach. Now, Rev. Wilson was about to determine Anne's guilt, and he did so without hesitation. He told Anne she had to leave the Boston church forever. When Anne stood up to leave, Mary was the only person who walked over and took Anne's hand. Mary had made her choice. She would stand by her friend.

The two women walked out of church together.

But Mary didn't just leave the church that day. Anne had been banished from Boston and the Massachusetts Bay Colony. Now Mary also had to find a new home. She may have liked Boston, but she liked her friend more. Mary always showed great loyalty to her friends no matter how much trouble they were in. Sometimes it got Mary in trouble, too, but she would not give up her fight to bring religious freedom to everyone, even if it cost her her life.

EARLY LIFE

Very little is known about Mary's early life. She may have been born in 1611 near London, England. She had a brother named William Barrett, but no one knows who her parents were. According to one story, her mother was Lady Arbella Stuart (sometimes spelled Arabella). Lady Stuart was first cousin to King James I, the ruler of England. If James died, Arbella could become queen. Many men tried to marry Arbella hoping to become king. James worried that Arbella was plotting to take over the throne and refused to let her marry.

But in 1610, Arbella fell in love with Sir William Seymour, the Duke of Somerset, and married him in secret. When James found out, he was furious and sent Arbella to Highgate prison. He locked William in the Tower of London, where the worst criminals were sent. Arbella escaped Highgate disguised as a man, but was captured as she boarded a boat for France. This time, King James locked her in the Tower of London, too. What the king did not know was that Lady Arbella had given birth to a daughter named Mary before she was arrested. In order to hide her daughter from the king, Arbella let her lady-in-waiting, named Mary Dyer, raise the young Mary as her own.

Four years later, Arbella died. William escaped

Lady Arbella Stuart

*Sir William Seymour
2nd Duke of Somerset*

prison and fled to France. He returned to England after King James died in 1625, when his daughter, Mary, was fourteen years old.

It's a good story, but most historians do not believe it because Mary's childhood name was Barrett, not Dyer. She didn't become Mary Dyer until she married William Dyer in 1633.

One thing that is known about Mary's childhood happened when she was fourteen. Mary visited the court of King Charles I, who became king when his father, James I, died. Mary wore a white satin ball gown stitched with gold and silver thread and embroidered with butterflies, grasshoppers and flowers. This dress was so special to Mary that when she moved to America several years later, she brought the dress with her. Today, pieces of the dress are owned by her descendants.

On October 27, 1633, when Mary was 22, she married William Dyer. He was two years older than her and a successful merchant. William was the son of a wealthy farmer, but at fourteen, he was trained to sell fish in the marketplace. He did not like that job very much, so by the time he married Mary, William was working as a milliner selling leather clothes like gloves and capes. He also sold knives, swords and jewelry. He was called a milliner because he imported fancy goods from the city of Milan, Italy.

Mary and William were married at St. Martin's-in-the-Field, a church in a field outside London. They were both Puritans, which was dangerous. Puritans wanted to reform, or "purify," the Anglican Church, the official religion of England. The Anglican Church was so powerful it was run by the king, but Puritans thought Anglicans were not worshipping God the right way. Many Puritans were beaten, sent to jail or executed just for speaking out against the Anglican Church. Some traveled to America to escape such brutal treatment, but Mary and her husband did not run away. They stayed in England to start a family.

Almost one year later, on October 24, 1634, Mary had her first baby. She named him William, after his father. Unfortunately, he was very sick and died three days later. William and Mary had been married exactly one year.

Mary was devastated, and she blamed the city for her son's death. She thought London was too dirty and crowded to raise a healthy child. She wanted to move to America with the other Puritans. When Mary became pregnant with her second child in 1635, she told William she wanted to leave England. William was having trouble selling his expensive goods and wanted to start a new business in America.

He agreed with Mary and sold all his land in England to pay for their trip.

In the spring of 1635, Mary, William, and several servants boarded a ship for the Massachusetts Bay Colony in America. Mary was five months pregnant. They sailed through rough seas and several storms, but they finally arrived in Boston four months later. Mary was now nine months pregnant with her second child and ready to begin her new life.

London in 1611

The Tower of London

When Mary Dyer was born, London was an important city of 75,000 people. The Tower of London soared above the skyline, but the streets were crowded and dirty, and people were dying from the plague. The city had hundreds of shops and several public schools. It also had the Globe Theater, where actors performed the works of William Shakespeare, the greatest playwright who ever lived. King James I published the King James Bible, and Sir Francis Bacon was teaching scientists the proper way to conduct experiments.

Unfortunately, many religious groups were fighting in the city. This is one reason the Puritans came to America: to practice their faith the way they wanted.

BANISHED FROM BOSTON

William and Mary arrived in Boston in early October, 1635. The Puritans who lived there welcomed them and their newborn son. Mary gave birth to Samuel on October 20th, right after the Dyers landed. A few days later, the Reverend Wilson baptized him into the Puritan church.

Mary liked Boston. It was much cleaner than London, and she felt Samuel would grow up healthy. It had a park for everyone to use and the first public school in America where Samuel could learn to read and write. Mary had been given a good education in London and felt it was extremely important for her son to attend a regular school.

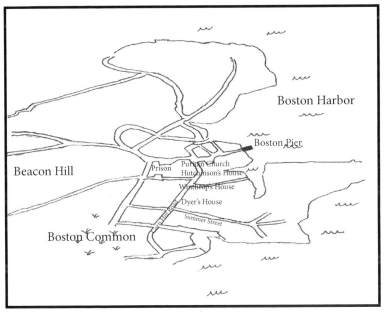

Boston in 1635

William built a five-room house with a six-foot-wide fireplace at the corner of Corn Hill Road and Summer Street on the edge of town. Mary kept a small vegetable garden and fruit trees in the yard and quickly made friends with many of the women in Boston. They got together to talk, knit, clean one another's homes and make apple butter and soap. Of all the women Mary met, she liked Anne Hutchinson the most. Mary even believed God brought her to Boston just to meet Anne.

Each morning at 9:00 a.m., village leaders banged

on a drum, calling everyone to church. If you did not go, you had to pay a fine. On Sunday, church lasted the entire day. When William and Mary wanted to join the church, they had to study the Bible and were questioned for hours about their beliefs. After two months of studying, they were finally given permission to join the Puritan church. This gave William the right to vote in elections, but not Mary, because women were not allowed to vote. She was not happy about this but could not change the law.

The Ten Commandments

The law was very strict. Men and women were kept apart at church and in all public places, and if anyone violated the Ten Commandments, they could be put to death.

William, however, was becoming an important person in Boston. He owned part of the Boston dock where ships landed, and in March, 1636, he was declared a Freeman. This meant that he could run for office. In 1637, William was elected town clerk and given more land. William had grown up as a farmer and used the land to raise more crops and keep hogs and goats for food. The land had four ponds and a river, where William liked to go fishing. At night, William and Mary sat and talked. Unlike many men at the time, William encouraged Mary to discuss important issues, and there was a lot to talk about. Mary did not like that women and poor people were not allowed to vote. She thought everyone should have a say in the way Boston was run.

Mary also did not like what happened to her friend, Roger Williams, right after the Dyers reached Boston. Roger thought the English settlers should treat the native Narragansett like equals and never take their land without paying for it. He also thought people should not be forced to go to church, and that the punishment for breaking the Ten Commandments was too severe. Mary particularly liked his ideas about separating church and state. She felt that if the Puritan Church did not run Boston, more people could vote.

Unfortunately, Roger's ideas were not very popular with most people in Boston, including Governor John Haynes. He asked the Freemen to vote on whether Roger could stay in Massachusetts. They voted by placing either a kernel of corn or a bean in a bowl. Corn meant he would be banished; a bean meant he could stay. No one knows how William Dyer voted, but only one bean was placed in the

Roger Williams

Roger Williams was born in London in 1603. He was educated at Cambridge University and spoke six languages. He once helped the famous writer, John Milton, learn Dutch. Roger and his wife, Mary, were among the first settlers to arrive in Boston in 1631. He became a Puritan minister.

Roger was America's first **abolitionist** and thought slavery should be banned everywhere in the New World. He also believed that the church should not control the government. This belief got him in trouble, and he was forced to leave Boston. He founded the city of Providence, Rhode Island, and started the first Baptist Church in America.

His third child was the first person born in Providence, Rhode Island, so he named her Providence!

Roger Williams meeting with the Narragansett

bowl. Roger Williams had been banished from Boston. Governor Haynes was so concerned that Roger's followers would support him that he sent soldiers to escort him out of Massachusetts. By the time they reached Roger's house, he had escaped into the woods.

Mary continued going to church. Her favorite minister was John Cotton. He spoke every Sunday afternoon. Mary liked the way he stressed the importance of faith rather than the law. She and Anne Hutchinson talked about his sermons after church or the next day. Soon, she and other women met at Anne's house every Monday to talk about Reverend Cotton's sermons. William Dyer became the first man to join the group and asked other men to sit with them.

Anne presented many of her ideas at these meetings. She said that men and women were equal before God, that Native Americans should not be slaves, and that strong faith was more

Anne Hutchinson on Trial

important than following the law. To prove it, Anne

helped people study the Bible without the aid of a minister, which was against the law.

The new governor, Henry Vane, liked Anne and supported her Free Grace Movement. Even though Anne was charged with breaking the law in 1636, he never put her on trial. When Vane was voted out of office in May, 1637, his replacement, Governor John Winthrop, decided Anne and her antinomian followers should be tried. Among those he convicted before Anne was William Dyer. He said William had been "infected by Anne Hutchinson's errors," like he had gotten a terrible disease! Governor Winthrop then banished him from Boston.

When Anne's trial began, Winthrop made himself both prosecutor and judge. This meant he would accuse Anne of her crimes and then decide if he was right. This was against the law, too, but Winthrop did it anyway.

Anne Hutchinson and John Winthrop lived across the street from each other. They saw each other almost every day!

One of the first things Governor Winthrop did was move the trial from Boston to Newtowne,

Massachusetts. He knew the people of Boston liked Anne, and he feared a jury from there might not find her guilty. Newtowne was far enough away that most people from Boston would never go there. To reach Newtowne, people had to take a ferryboat across the Charles River and then walk five miles through the woods where wild animals still lived.

Anne's trial began on November 7, 1637. A very bad snowstorm struck Massachusetts just before the trial started. Many people gave up trying to get to Newtowne, but not Mary. She put on a heavy wool coat, mittens and boots and walked two miles to the ferry landing. She had to walk. The snow was too deep for horses.

When Anne's trial began, Governor Winthrop discovered he was not a good lawyer and could not prove his case against Anne. Finally, as judge, he declared that her Free Grace Movement was an illegal group. He then let his deputy governor, Thomas Dudley, prosecute her. Dudley was a professional lawyer and he attacked Anne's religious beliefs, claiming she said untrue things about church leaders. When Anne tried to defend herself, Winthrop refused to let her speak in court because she was a woman. Anne was losing the trial.

Winthrop gave her one night to change her beliefs,

but Anne did not give up. That night, she met with lawyers who supported her cause, and the next day, Anne went on the attack. Although she could not testify in court, she could question others and act as her own lawyer. She disproved many of Dudley's charges against her, but then Anne made a mistake. She criticized the church leaders in court, saying some of them were not fit to preach. Anne specifically mentioned the Reverend John Wilson, the powerful minister who founded the First Church in Boston. She also said that God had spoken to her when she lived in England. This offended many of the Puritans on the jury because they did not believe that God would talk with a woman or a person they believed had "poor faith."

When the trial ended, Anne was found guilty. Like Roger Williams, she was banished from Boston. Because winter was coming, Winthrop said she could leave in the spring. When Anne asked where she was to go, Winthrop said he didn't know, only that she could not stay in Massachusetts.

As Mary and Anne left the courtroom together, Governor Winthrop heard a woman say that Mary was guilty, too, because she was "the mother of a monster." Winthrop did not know what this meant, but he was determined to find out.

For Mary, it meant that her troubles were just beginning.

Anne Bradstreet
The Most Famous Woman in America

Anne Bradstreet (1612-1672) was the first woman in North America to have her writing published. Her poems were very popular in America and Europe. She wanted to attend the meetings at Anne Hutchinson's house, but her husband wouldn't let her. Anne Bradstreet eventually became the most famous woman in America when her poems were published in 1647, but in 1637, she couldn't save her friend from being banished.

MOTHER OF A MONSTER

On October 17, 1637, three weeks before Anne's trial began, Mary Dyer gave birth to her third child. Anne Hutchinson and another woman named Jane Hawkins rushed to Mary's house to help her. Jane's nickname was Goody and she was a midwife, or someone who helps women give birth. Unfortunately, Anne and Jane did not have good news. The baby was born two months early and did not survive. For the second time, Mary Dyer had lost a child.

Anne contacted the Reverend John Cotton, Mary's favorite minister. Along with Goody, they buried the baby girl in the middle of the night in the church cemetery. Although it was against the law to bury a deceased baby in secret in Boston, they thought it was for the best. The baby had many deformities, and Anne thought Governor Winthrop would see this as a punishment from God because Puritans believed that women who preached would give birth to deformed babies. They even thought women who heard women preach would have deformed children.

As it turned out, Anne was right to worry. She and Reverend Cotton kept the secret, but Goody did not. When Winthrop found out, he contacted Reverend Cotton. Cotton refused to lie and revealed where the baby was buried. Winthrop then ordered the baby dug up so he could see it. The ground, however, was frozen, so they had to wait. When people finally dug up Mary's daughter five months after she had been buried, the deformities looked far worse.

Winthrop described Mary's daughter as having four horns on top of her head, claws instead of hands, scales on her back, and two mouths. It is very likely the governor exaggerated the baby's appearance to make everyone think that Mary was being punished by God.

William Dyer did not know any of this. He was with several of Anne Hutchinson's followers looking for good land to start a new colony in Rhode Island. Roger Williams suggested an island with good farmland and fishing water. On March 27, 1638, they bought Aquidneck Island from the Wompanaug for forty white beads, ten winter coats and twenty hoes for farming. William rushed home to tell Mary the good news.

When he walked through the door he found Mary crying. Governor Winthrop had declared Mary to be the mother of a monster and said it was proof that she was a "heretic," or someone who doesn't believe religious teachings. Winthrop said God was punishing Mary for not being a good Puritan. Some people even claimed that the devil was the father of Mary's deceased baby.

Governor Winthrop told the Dyers to leave Massachusetts by May, but they didn't wait that long. They were eager to start a new life away from Boston. William sold his land and his share of Boston pier and, in late April, he, Mary, and two-year-old Samuel packed up everything they owned to move again.

The Puritans were so strict that today the word "puritanical" means having an unbending moral belief!

A ROUGH LIFE IN RHODE ISLAND

The Dyers thought Aquidneck Island was beautiful, but also scary. They had almost no food because their farm animals had been sent on a different boat and had not arrived yet. They also had no house to live in or use as shelter to hide from the wolves that roamed the land. Some of the antinomian families took shelter in caves before they built their homes, but William used a trick he learned from the Narragansett. He bent birch trees until they reached the ground, then made walls out of sticks and mud. The Dyers lived there until he built a house.

Soon, the Dyers' hogs and goats arrived, but the wolves hunted the animals and threatened to attack

The Narragansett

The death of Miantonomoh

The Narragansett were a powerful tribe in what is now called New England. They were so powerful that several small tribes paid the Narragansett to protect them from other tribes. When explorer Giovanni da Verrazano met the Narragansett in 1524, he described them as being ruled by powerful kings called sachem. Two of the most powerful sachem were Miantonomoh and Canonicus.

Narragansett money was called wampum. Purple shells or beads were worth more than white beads. In the winter, families lived in big buildings called longhouses, and in the summer, they lived in tents called wigwams. The Narragansett were loyal friends and developed a strong relationship with Roger Williams.

the settlers. At last Roger Williams came to the rescue. He arrived with 200 Narragansett warriors who drove the wolves off the island. As a thank-you present, the settlers gave their leader, Miantonomoh, sugar. They then finished building fences to keep their animals safe from any remaining wolves.

The settlers began building their town. Although the Narragansett called this area Pocasset, the settlers named it Portsmouth after a town in England. The citizens quickly elected their leaders and made William town secretary. He wrote many notes about their meetings and let Mary read them to make sure they were correct. She was happy to be involved in running Portsmouth, unlike Boston.

A few weeks after the settlers arrived, they received bad news. In May, Anne Hutchinson gave birth to a baby, who, like Mary's daughter, did not live. When John Winthrop heard the news back in Boston, he said that God was punishing Anne for her beliefs. He even said that the devil himself was the father, just like people said about Mary's baby. Winthrop sent letters to England and to several governors in America saying this proved that he had made the right decision in banishing Anne.

On June 1, the settlers got another scare. An earthquake struck the island. People reported seeing giant monsters walking among their sheep and worried that God was punishing them. They did not relax until they discovered that Boston had also felt the earthquake. They believed that God would not be punishing both them and the Puritans.

Still, the settlers were uneasy. Life on the island was difficult, and that summer their crops almost failed when snow flurries fell in August. Now, they were really worried that God was punishing them. It was supposed to be hot, but it was snowing!

The Little Ice Age

In the 1600s, the world was going through a mini Ice Age, which made the winters very cold and sometimes brought snow in the summer!

Mary began to think moving to Portsmouth was a mistake. The new governor, William Coddington, did not let women speak in church. He did not follow many of Anne Hutchinson's beliefs despite saying he would. Back in Boston, before the antinomians left,

Coddington was the first person to sign the Portsmouth Compact. This document said that Portsmouth would be run according to Christian beliefs but would not be run by church leaders. Mary felt he was not following the law, and she was growing unhappy.

Her husband, however, was once again successful. As secretary, he had been given ten extra acres of land, and William Coddington gave him his own, small island as a gift. It became known as Dyer Island, and William found it rich with clams, mussels, horseshoe crabs, and other shellfish. Even though crops were struggling, he could still find food for his family. William wanted to stay in Portsmouth.

All that was about to change. In late 1638, a man named Samuel Gorton arrived in Portsmouth from Boston. Like Mary, he thought men and women should be equal. He did not like what the Puritans preached, and hoped Portsmouth would be different. When he learned how strict Coddington was, he urged William Hutchinson, Anne's husband, to run for governor. Hutchinson agreed, and on April 28, 1639, he became the new governor. Anne and Mary were thrilled. They thought women would finally have a chance to participate in the way Portsmouth was run.

The Portsmouth Compact

On March 7, 1638, twenty-three men met in Boston to write and sign the Portsmouth Compact. This document created the town of Portsmouth, Rhode Island. It is an important document for two reasons:

1. Signed 138 years before the Declaration of Independence, it was the first time settlers established a colony in America without pledging allegiance to England.

2. Signed 153 years before the United States **Constitution**, it separated church and state. Colonists would be ruled by the government, not the church. The Compact let any Christian live in Portsmouth and worship God as he or she pleased.

For some unknown reason, four names were scratched off the Portsmouth Compact. Maybe the signers changed their minds about going to Portsmouth, but at least three of them took part in founding Newport a year later.

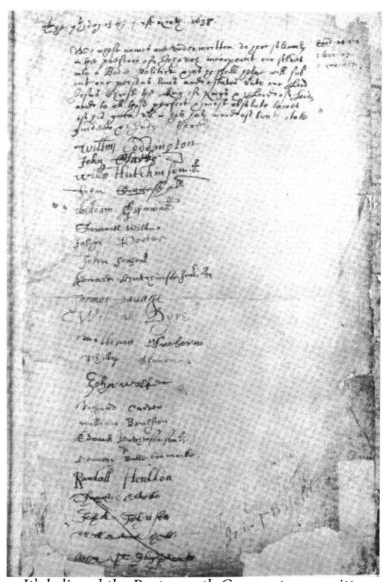

It's believed the Portsmouth Compact was written in William Dyer's handwriting.

William Coddington, however, was upset that he lost the election, and he left to start a new town on the southern part of Aquidneck Island. William Dyer had surveyed the land and knew it well. Since Coddington had been good to him, William felt he should join him in creating the new town. They called this town Newport.

Mary did not want to leave Anne, but she agreed to go with her husband to Newport. She even helped him with a secret plan to secure the land. As secretary, William kept the records of who owned which pieces of property. He did not want the people of Portsmouth telling them they could not settle where they wanted because the land was not theirs, so William came up with a trick to keep the land. Mary hid the deeds to all the properties between his shoulder blades. Once they were safely out of Portsmouth, William Coddington, William Dyer and the others claimed the land as their own!

In May, 1639, one year after they founded Portsmouth, the Dyers were building another new town. They moved to the southern tip of Aquidneck Island and once more lived in a house made of bent trees and mud. Mary missed Anne, but she was determined to make a good life for her family in a brand new town.

A NEW LIFE IN NEWPORT

Life in Newport was even harder for Mary than it had been in Portsmouth. The settlers built the town on the edge of a swamp. There was little food and the mosquitoes were so thick that Mary was covered in red welts. Her long dress, sleeves and bonnet were not enough to protect her.

Mary wanted to leave Newport and return to Portsmouth, but then she learned that the people of Boston had forgiven the antinomians and invited them to come back. Mary thought it was a good idea. She wanted to continue her friendship with the Reverend John Cotton. William, however, refused. He thought he could be a success in Newport. Once

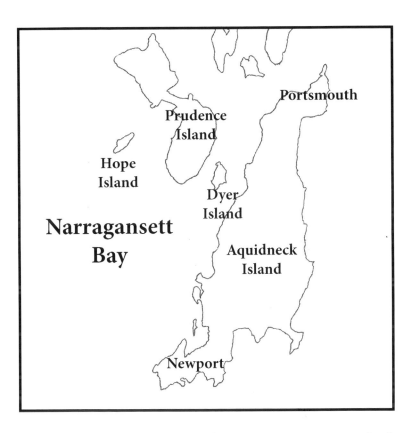

again, he had been elected town secretary. He had a lot of land and an entire island for hunting and fishing.

But the other settlers were not so sure. Like Mary, some of them wanted to go back to Boston. Just as life was becoming unbearable for the settlers, the Narragansett came to their rescue again. They drained the swamp and replaced the muck with sand and gravel. This got rid of many of the mosquitoes and other bugs that bothered the people of Newport. The Narragansett did all that work for just twelve brass buttons.

Mary did not have many friends in Newport. When she lived in Boston, Mary loved talking with the other women and going to Anne's house on Mondays, but only a few families lived in Newport. To find friends, Mary visited the Narragansett. It was a decision that changed her life. She discovered she liked the way they lived. Women were important in the daily lives of the Narragansett. While the men did the hunting and fishing, the women were in charge of farming. Mary had her small garden and loved growing vegetables, but she learned a lot more about farming from the Narragansett women. She also liked that even the men of Newport had to ask the Narragansett women for help when it came to raising crops.

The Narragansett showed the settlers how to grow peas, beans, corn, wheat and pumpkins. They taught them how to make fertilizer from animal manure, seaweed and leftover fish. Mary's hands smelled awful, but she knew her family would have plenty of food in the fall.

Mary was also interested in the religion of the Narragansett. She discovered they believed many of the things Anne Hutchinson did. Religion was not forced on anyone. People were free to practice as they wished. Mary also agreed with their belief that God existed and that every person had a part of God in him or her.

Mary enjoyed her visits with the Narragansett and could not understand why William Coddington did not trust them. Governor Coddington would not let the Narragansett hunt or fish on land owned by the town of Newport. She found the Narragansett to be nice, and she valued their friendship, just like Roger Williams did.

A longhouse

As much as Mary liked her new friends, she still missed Anne, and it turned out Anne missed her. Anne asked her husband to use his power as governor to make amends with the people of Newport and reunite the two colonies. William Hutchinson agreed and set up a meeting with William Coddington.

The two men decided the colonies should rejoin and keep the name Portsmouth. Mary was thrilled. Even though Anne still lived on the other side of the island, she could visit her without anyone getting angry.

But her joy did not last long. Two years later, in 1642, Anne's husband died. Anne was not very popular in Portsmouth. People questioned her faith, just like they did in Boston. Before they could ban Anne and her children, she left. Anne moved to New Netherland, in an area known today as the Bronx in New York City. The area was controlled by the Dutch, not the English. Anne thought they would accept her religious beliefs. She also hoped to convert the local Siwanoy to Christianity.

Unfortunately, one year later, Anne was murdered. Mary was horrified by the news and felt more alone than ever. Once again, her life was about to go in a new direction.

The Death of Anne Hutchinson

The murder of Anne Hutchinson and her family

Anne Hutchinson and seven of her children arrived in New Netherland in the summer of 1642.

William Kieft, the local governor, was arguing with the Siwanoy chief, Wampage. Wampage believed that Kieft cheated the Siwanoy out of land, and he wanted the Dutch settlers out of Siwanoy territory.

Anne tried to develop a good relationship with the Siwanoy, just as she had with the Narragansett, but failed. In August, 1643, Siwanoy warriors raided the Dutch settlement. All the settlers except Anne and her family fled.

The Siwanoy asked Anne to tie up her dogs. Her daughter Francis did, and that's when the warriors attacked. They killed Anne, six of her children, her son-in-law, and several servants. They also killed the cattle and burned down the house.

The only one to escape was Anne's nine-year-old daughter, Susanna. She was out picking berries. When she heard the screaming, she hid inside a split rock, but the warriors found her. Some people say they did not kill Susanna because they liked her red hair and nicknamed her Autumn Leaf. Whatever the reason, the Siwanoy took Susanna to live with them.

Two years later, the Siwanoy sold Susanna back to her older brother and sister in Boston. Susanna grew up and had eleven children. Three of her descendants—Stephen Douglas (1860), George Romney (1968), and Mitt Romney (2012)—even ran for president!

> *While three of Susanna's descendants ran for president, three of Anne's from her other children actually became president—Franklin D. Roosevelt (1933-1945), George Herbert Walker Bush (1989-1993), and George W. Bush (2001-2009)!*

MARY BECOMES A QUAKER

A few weeks after Anne Hutchinson died, Mary Dyer gave birth to her third son. She named him Mahershalalhashbaz ("Ma-her-shal-hash-baz") in honor of her friend. His name means "suddenly attacked, quickly taken" in Hebrew, the language of the Old Testament. Everyone called him Maher, for short.

Mary was determined to continue Anne's work, and looked for a religion that supported women's rights. Roger Williams had become a Baptist and was preaching that women should wear veils. Even her own husband seemed to be against her. In 1647, William helped Rhode Island Governor John

Coggeshall write a new Code of Laws. The law gave men the right to free speech, but not women. Mary opposed the new law, but it was a big help to William. In 1650, Coggeshall appointed him Rhode Island's first attorney general. In fact, William was the first attorney general anywhere in the colonies. His job was to make sure the law was followed.

Mary's Children

1. **William (born 1634)**
2. **Samuel (1635)**
3. **Stillborn daughter (1637)**
4. **William (1640)**
5. **Mahershalalhashbaz (1643)**
6. **Henry (1647)**
7. **Mary (before 1650)**
8. **Charles (1650)**

William took his job as attorney general very seriously. He expected everyone to follow the law. In 1651, his old friend William Coddington took over four towns and set himself up as governor for life.

This meant he was in charge of the towns for as long as he liked and could not be voted out of office. William thought this was against Rhode Island law and traveled to England with Roger Williams to ask the English government to take away some of Coddington's power. William won his case, and Governor Coddington was replaced.

But when William returned to Rhode Island later that year, he had bad news for Mary. John Winthrop's letters had been published in England and everyone was talking about her and Anne Hutchinson's babies. People were saying they were the mothers of monsters and that Anne's death was a punishment from God for not being a good Christian.

Mary desperately wanted to sail to England to defend her friend, and a few months later, in January, 1652, she got her chance. William had to go back to London, and Mary went with him. She planned to tell people that Anne was a good person and a good Christian.

This trip changed William's and Mary's lives forever.

The English Civil War had just ended, but England was about to enter a new war with the Netherlands. Parliament made William a navy captain, asking him to fight in the First Anglo-Dutch War (1652-

British and Dutch warships fighting in 1652

1654). William quickly returned to America to unite the English colonies against the Dutch settlers. He became a privateer, a sort of pirate. In exchange for attacking Dutch ships, forts and towns, William would be allowed to keep a portion of any treasure he captured.

Mary, however, stayed in England to study religion under George Fox, the leader of a new religion called the Quakers. She found that the Quakers supported women's rights and believed many of the things Anne did. They even made Mary a minister, something the Puritans would never do.

The Quakers were also **pacifists**, meaning they did

not believe in fighting wars. Mary was distraught that while she was preaching peace, her husband was fighting the Dutch, but she could not stop him. He was so successful as a navy captain, the New England colonies promoted him to Commander-in-Chief Upon the Sea. William was now in charge of the entire northern naval war against New Netherland, which today we call New York.

Wall Street

The Dutch were so worried about William Dyer attacking the city of New Amsterdam (now New York City) that they built a long wall to protect it. They called the road next to it Wall Street. Today, that street is the center for banking around the world!

In 1657, three years after the war ended, Mary came home to preach in America. The Quakers had arrived in the colonies a year earlier, and like other non-Puritan groups in Massachusetts, were not very popular. The government in Boston passed many laws against the Quakers. Any Quaker who

Religious Society of Friends founder George Fox

preached could be put in jail, Quaker women could be whipped and men could have their ears cut off. George Fox told his followers to be pleasant to everyone they met and not fight back. Most of all, he told them to keep preaching. Unable to stop them, Massachusetts leaders did not just make it illegal for Quakers to preach—they made it illegal to be a Quaker at all.

Mary did not know this because she was on a ship sailing across the Atlantic Ocean. When her ship arrived in Boston, she and a widow named Anne Burden, who had come to pay her dead husband's debts, were asked if they were Quakers. Both women said yes. Before they could get off the ship, they were arrested. The judge declared them guilty, even though the law was passed while they were at sea. He threw Mary in a tiny cell with wooden boards

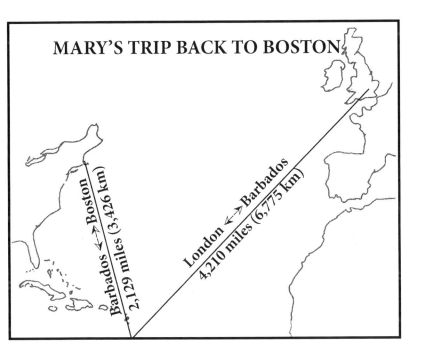

MARY'S TRIP BACK TO BOSTON

Barbados ↔ Boston (3,426 km)
2,129 miles

London ↔ Barbados
4,210 miles (6,775 km)

over the windows. There was no bed, so Mary had to sleep on the dirt floor. They burned her Quaker books and wouldn't even let her write a letter to her husband to tell him where she was. Finally, Mary managed to get some paper and slipped a letter through a crack in the boards. The person who took it agreed to send it to William.

When William learned his wife was in prison, he went to Boston and barged into Governor Endecott's house. He complained that Mary was being treated worse than a dog because at least dogs were given a fireplace to curl up next to and straw to sleep on. Mary had been in prison for ten weeks before Endecott ordered her set free as a favor to William since he was Rhode Island's attorney general, a war hero, and a Puritan. But William had to promise to take Mary straight out of Massachusetts without stopping anywhere to spend the night. Mary was even banned from talking to anyone!

William also had to promise that Mary would never return to Massachusetts or she would face an even greater penalty, possibly being whipped, tied up and dragged behind a horse, or executed.

At first, Mary kept her husband's promise not to return and only preached in Rhode Island. She then preached for several months in New Haven, Connecticut. The governor, John Winthrop, Jr.—the son of the man who had banished Anne Hutchinson and the antinomians from Boston—arrested Mary and expelled her from the colony to stop her from preaching.

But Mary kept going. She believed she had the right to preach anywhere she wanted. In June, 1659, she learned that authorities had arrested three men and an eleven-year-old girl named Patience Scott for teaching Quaker beliefs in Massachusetts. Mary walked thirty-nine miles through the woods, along

*William Penn signing a treaty with the
Lenape in 1683, leading to the
creation of Pennsylvania*

an old Narragansett trail, carrying only food and some bedding to sleep on. After several days, she reached the prison. As she tried to comfort her friends, the guards arrested Mary for being a Quaker.

William Dyer quickly wrote a letter to the court saying that, as a lawyer, he often visited people in prison and was never thrown in jail, so his wife shouldn't be either. The court ignored William and put Mary on trial.

The Quakers

The Quakers are also known as the Religious Society of Friends. They were founded by George Fox in England sometime in the 1640s. The name "Quaker" comes from the idea that one should tremble or "quake" before the word of God.

The Quakers believe that church and state should be separate, and that the government should not tell religious groups what to do. They also believe that men and women are equal before God and in all church activities. They teach that people can talk with God without a minister and are guided by an "inner light," or a piece of God, found in the soul. Quakers are pacifists who believe all people should live in peace.

Perhaps the most famous Quaker in America was William Penn (1644-1718), who founded Philadelphia ("The City of Brotherly Love") and the Commonwealth of Pennsylvania ("Penn's Woods"). Quaker settlements in New Jersey, Pennsylvania, and Delaware became famous for letting Christians, Jews, and Muslims live together and practice their faiths without government interference.

Mary Dyer leading a Quaker prayer meeting

In mid-September, Mary and the others stood before a judge. Mary argued that people had the right to their own religious beliefs and that she wanted to keep the judge and her jailers from "shedding innocent blood." The judge disagreed and gave her and the other adults two days to leave Massachusetts and never return or they would be executed. Patience, who was Anne Hutchinson's niece, was set free for being too young to be charged with a crime.

Mary and two of the men, Marmaduke Stephenson and William Robinson, waited just three weeks before returning to Massachusetts. Mary went to Boston, where she was immediately arrested for preaching. When Stephenson and Robinson heard about Mary's arrest, they traveled to Boston to join her. They were quickly arrested, too. This time, Governor John Endecott oversaw their trial. On October 19, 1659, he asked each of them if they were the Quakers who had been banished before. Each said yes, and Endecott quickly sentenced them to be taken to the "place of execution and there hang till you be dead."

As Mary was led from the courtroom, she replied, "Yea, and joyfully I go."

Mary was willing to die for her beliefs, but her husband was determined to save her life.

The English Civil War

The English Civil War (1642-1651) took place between two groups—the Parliamentarians, who wanted more democracy, and the Royalists, who supported King Charles I. The Parliamentarians wanted to establish a constitutional monarchy. This meant the king could only rule England if Parliament said he could. The king's supporters believed God picked the king to rule and Parliament could not change that. The Parliamentarians executed Charles I in 1649 before defeating King Charles II's army in 1651. They banished Charles II from the country.

Oliver Cromwell

Charles II

Oliver Cromwell led the Parliamentarians. As a Puritan, he ended the Church of England's rule over the country's religion. He supported letting most Protestants worship freely. The Parliamentarians were nicknamed Roundheads because they cut their hair in a bowl shape, making their heads look round!

When Cromwell died in 1658, the king's supporters, known as Cavaliers, attacked the Roundheads and in May, 1660, made Charles II king again.

HANGED AS A FLAG

Eight days after Mary was sentenced to die, the marshal escorted her out of prison. It was October 27, 1659, Mary's twenty-sixth wedding anniversary. But instead of spending the day with her husband, Mary was silently preparing to be hanged. She stood alongside fellow Quakers Marmaduke Stephenson and William Robinson. The men were clapped in iron chains and marched to their deaths while soldiers beat on drums. Mary reached over and took her friends' hands as she walked between them. The marshal was offended that she held the hand of any man who was not her husband, but Mary would not let go. She said she was happy to hold their hands since they would soon enjoy "the spirit of the Lord" in heaven.

Mary and her fellow Quakers approached the Great Elm tree in the Boston Common where all prisoners were hanged. William Robinson climbed a ladder, and a rope was placed around his neck. He then gave a short speech saying he was willing to die for his beliefs, but the drums beat louder and attempted to drown him out. The Reverend John Wilson also shouted at him, telling him to be quiet

Mary prepares to die as William Robinson and Marmaduke Stephenson hang above her.

or else he would "die with a lie in his mouth." Finally, the hangman silenced Robinson by tightening the noose and letting him swing from the branch.

Marmaduke Stephenson went next. He also gave a short speech before being hanged. When it was Mary's turn, the executioner put a rope around her neck, bound her hands and placed a handkerchief over her face. The handkerchief belonged to the Rev. Wilson, the same man who had banished Anne Hutchinson twenty-two years before. Once Mary climbed the ladder, the hangman tied her dress to her legs so it wouldn't fly up. Mary quietly prayed and prepared to die. But seconds before the executioner could hang her, Mary's oldest son, Samuel, raced through the crowd on a white horse. He waved a piece of **parchment** signed by Governor Endecott saying Mary could live!

Governor John Endecott

At first, Mary did not believe it and refused to climb down the ladder. People shouted for the guards to bring her down, but Mary called for them to be quiet so she could ask God what to do. People tried to pull her off the ladder to keep her from being hanged. Finally, the marshal lifted her from the ladder and carried her back to jail so her husband could take her back to Rhode Island.

What Mary did not know was that Governor Endecott never wanted to execute her. No woman had ever died for her religious beliefs in America, and he did not want Mary to be the first. He even signed the pardon before Samuel reached his office. He had received letters from her husband and supporters saying Mary should not die simply for acting like a Quaker. Even John Winthrop, Jr., who banned Mary from preaching in New Haven, Connecticut, wrote to Endecott saying he was willing to get on his knees and beg for Mary's life. Winthrop did not want her preaching, but he also did not want her to die.

So Endecott arranged for Mary to be saved. He told the executioner to hang her last so she could watch her friends die. He thought this would scare her away from ever preaching in Massachusetts again. He even made sure that her son arrived at the last second. Once Mary was back in prison, Endecott ruled that she had forty-eight hours to leave the colony and never return or she would hang like her friends.

Mary, however, refused the governor's pardon. She wrote a letter to the court saying that they had executed two innocent men and she would rather join them in death than live among the guilty. People were impressed by Mary's bravery and asked that she be given a full pardon. Worried that the citizens of Boston would take her side and call for the laws against the Quakers to be repealed, officials put Mary on a horse and led her out of town. Along the way, she was forced to pass the hanging bodies of Marmaduke Stephenson and William Robinson as a reminder of what would happen to her if she returned. Once Mary reached the Rhode Island border, she was given over to another man who stayed with her until she was far away from Boston.

But Mary did not want to return to Massachusetts right away. She joined other Quakers on Shelter Island in New York, preaching to Native Americans like Anne Hutchinson had done. She left after six months, but did not go home to her husband or six children in Rhode Island. She knew that William would stop her from carrying out her plan: Mary was going to Boston to ask Governor Endecott to change the law that kept people from joining whatever religion they wanted.

Mary arrived in Boston sometime in April, 1660,

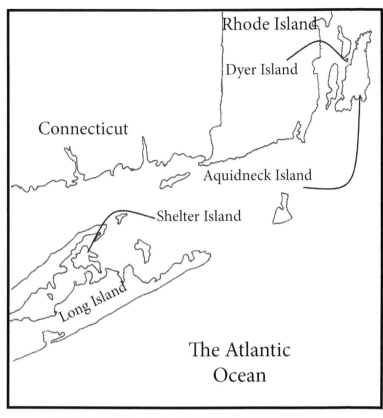

Rhode Island

Dyer Island

Connecticut

Aquidneck Island

Shelter Island

Long Island

The Atlantic
Ocean

MARY'S TRIP TO SHELTER ISLAND

where she spent a few weeks visiting friends and supporters. Finally, on May 21, Mary approached the prison where she had been locked up. She asked the guards if she could comfort the Quaker prisoners being held there. The guards immediately arrested her and took her back to court.

Governor John Endecott

John Endecott was among the first Puritans to come to America in 1628. He led his expedition and founded the town of Salem, Massachusetts. Unfortunately for him, the settlers started arguing with one another, and by 1630, Endecott was no longer governor.

Endecott was appointed to assist the new governor, John Winthrop, but eventually became a military officer, where he used his soldiers to attack Native American tribes. He nearly wiped out the Pequots in the 1630s. In 1649, he became governor again. He remained governor for most of the rest of his life before dying in 1665.

Endecott wanted the Puritans to separate from the Church of England. He did not tolerate groups who disagreed with the Puritans. In addition to arresting Quakers, he did not like Catholics. He once tore up the British flag because the red cross on it reminded him of the pope! Although he hanged Mary Dyer, he was good friends with Roger Williams and offered him protection from those who banished Williams from Boston.

Mary brought before Governor Endecott

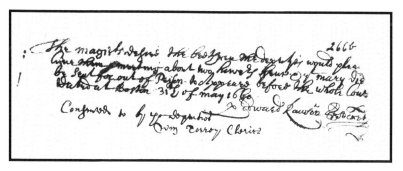

The warrant for Mary's arrest in 1660.

Ten days later, Mary stood before Governor Endecott. He asked Mary if she was still a Quaker. When Mary said yes, the governor said she would be executed the next day. Mary then asked Endecott and the court to "repeal your unrighteous laws." If they did not, she said others would come to protest them.

Governor Endecott had heard enough. He yelled, "Away with her!" and Mary was led from the courtroom back to her cell. William Dyer wrote one last letter to the governor, begging him to pardon his wife again. He said that he would be forever grateful if the governor would show her compassion and mercy. But Endecott was no longer listening. He thought that if he did not execute Mary this time, she would never stop preaching in Massachusetts.

On June 1, 1660, at 9:00 a.m., Mary was once more taken to the Great Elm tree* to be hanged. People gathered outside her prison cell and lined the street to speak with her, begging her to repent. As the drums beat, armed men surrounded Mary and led her to the Boston Common. Mary calmly climbed the ladder by herself, but did not show fear as the noose was placed around her neck. Instead, she gave a small smile to the crowd as if to say she was ready to die for her beliefs. The Reverend John Wilson— who baptized Mary's son nearly twenty-five years ago—told Mary that if she climbed down the ladder and returned home, she might be allowed to live, but Mary said no, that her cause was just and that her executioners were guilty.

Reverend Wilson then asked Mary to repent for her crimes and ask God for forgiveness. He wanted her to claim she had been tricked by the devil, but again Mary refused. She said, "Nay, man, I shall not now repent." Those were her last words. With nothing else to say, the executioner tightened the rope and at last hanged Mary Dyer.

*Some accounts say Mary was not hanged from the Great Elm but rather a nearby oak tree.

Humphrey Atherton, a Puritan judge who did not like Quakers, looked at her body and said, "Mary Dyer did hang as a flag for others to take example by." And as Atherton predicted, the colonists were inspired by Mary's death, but not in the way he expected.

THE MEN WHO HANGED MARY DYER

JOHN WEBB

Captain of the Guard John Webb died while hunting whales in 1668. He got caught in a rope and was pulled into the ocean, where he drowned.

EDWARD WANTON

A year after Mary's death, the officer of the gallows became a Quaker. Three years later he was arrested for preaching, but his life was spared.

Mary Dyer being led to the gallows for the final time

MARY DYER'S LEGACY

After Mary was hanged, Quakers and other religious groups the Puritans did not like protested the laws against religious freedom. They followed Mary's brave example and stood up to **tyranny**. They were inspired by her words that "My life not availeth me in comparison to the liberty of the truth." She meant that her life was less important than doing the right thing.

Unfortunately, Governor Endecott would not change the law and continued to whip and imprison Quakers. Another Quaker, William Leddra, was hanged in 1661. He, William Robinson, Marmaduke

Stephenson, and Mary Dyer became known as the Boston **Martyrs**. But his death, like Mary's, only convinced people to fight for the right to worship as they pleased.

Back in England, King Charles II, the son of the king Mary met when she was fourteen, did not like all the religious troubles in Massachusetts. Mary's death bothered him deeply, and he ordered the Puritans to stop executing Quakers. He then sent soldiers to Massachusetts to protect them. In 1684, he went further, and revoked Massachusetts' charter, or its right to rule itself.

When Charles II died in 1685, his brother, James II, became king. James was a Catholic and did not like the way the Puritans treated them. In 1686, he sent a royal governor to rule Massachusetts. In 1689, the English Parliament passed the Toleration Acts that protected religious freedom for all Protestants, though Catholics and people of other religions were not protected from discrimination.

After America gained independence from England and the Founding Fathers passed the Constitution in 1789, they made religious tolerance the law of the land as part of the First **Amendment**. One of those Founding Fathers, Thomas Jefferson, was so proud of a law he wrote in 1777 guaranteeing

The First Amendment

The First Amendment is the first additional law to the Constitution of the United States. It became the law of the land in December, 1791. It is very short, but provides many important freedoms for Americans. The entire First Amendment says:

The **Bill of Rights,** *or the first ten amendments*

"Congress shall make no law respecting an establishment of religion, or prohibiting the free exercise thereof; or abridging the freedom of speech, or of the press; or the right of the people peaceably to assemble, and to **petition** *the Government for a redress of grievances."*

The first line says the government shall not establish an official religion. This means church and state must remain separate. It then says that people can practice any religion they want, or no religion at all. Mary Dyer was fighting for the right to religious freedom more than 130 years before it became law!

freedom of religion for people in Virginia that he had it listed on his tombstone, right after writing The Declaration of Independence.

Mary Dyer did not live to see these changes, but her death began a revolution no one could stop. October 27th, the day that she, William Robinson, and Marmaduke Stephenson were scheduled to die, is now celebrated as International Religious Freedom Day. Even Massachusetts declared her a hero. In 1959, nearly 300 years after her death, they erected a statue of her in front of the Massachusetts State House in Boston. Now, the Massachusetts governor has to pass Mary whenever he goes to work!

Copies of that statue are located at the Friends Center in Philadelphia, the city founded by Quaker William Penn, and on the campus of Earlham College in Indiana, a school started by Quakers in 1847.

And in Rhode Island, people can rest at Founders' Brook Park in Portsmouth at a garden dedicated to Anne Hutchinson and Mary Dyer, or learn about Dyer Island's role in preserving the wildlife of Narragansett Bay. No one roams Dyer Island anymore, but the people of Portsmouth have not forgotten Mary's fight to bring religious freedom to everyone.

The Mary Dyer statue in front of the Massachusetts State House

LETTERS FROM WILLIAM & MARY

Editor's note: All writing, including misspelled words and names, belongs to the authors. The spelling of some words has changed over time, while others simply appear to be spelled incorrectly. In a few places, punctuation (and one or two words) have been adjusted so that a reader today can more easily understand the meaning or intent of these letters.

William Dyer's Letter to the Boston Magistrates
August 30, 1659

Gentlemen:

Having received some letters from my wife, I am given to understand of her commitment to close prison to a place (according to description) not unlike Bishop Bonner's* rooms... It is a sad condition, in executing such cruelties towards their fellow creatures and sufferers... Had you no commiseration of a tender soul that being wett to the skin, you cause her to thrust into a room whereon was nothing to sitt or lye down upon but dust... had your dogg been wett you would have offered it the liberty of a chimney corner to dry itself, or had your hoggs been pend in a sty, you would have offered them some dry straw, or else you would have wanted mercy to your beast, but alas Christians now with you are used worse [than] hoggs or doggs... oh merciless cruelties.

*Bishop Edmund Bonner (c1500-1569) arrested and tortured non-Catholics in England, earning him the nickname Bloody Bonner.

71

You have done more in persecution in one year than the worst bishops did in seven, and now to add more towards a tender woman... that gave you no just cause against her for did she come to your meeting to disturb them as you call itt, or did she come to reprehend the magistrates? [She] only came to visit her friends in prison and when dispatching that her intent of returning to her family as she declared in her [statement] the next day to the Governor, therefore it is you that disturbed her, else why was she not let alone. [What] house entered she to molest or what did she, that like a malefactor she must be hauled to [prison] or what law did she transgress? She was about a business justifiable before God and all good men.

The worst of men, the bishops themselves, denied not the visitation and release of friends to their prisoners, which myself hath often experienced by visiting Mr. Prine, Mr. Smart and other eminent [men] yea, when he was commanded close in the towne, I had resort once or twice a week and [I was] never fetched before authority to ask me wherefore I came to the towne, or Kings bench, or Gatehouse... had there not been more adventurours tender hearted professors than yo'selves many of them you call godly ministers and others might have perished...

if that course you take had been in use with them, as to send for a person and ask them whe'fore they came thither. What hath not people in America the same liberty as beasts and birds to pass the land or air without examination?

Have you a law that says the light in M. Dyre is not M. Dyre's rule, if you have for that or any the fornamed a law, she may be made a transgresso', for words and your mittimus hold good, but if not, then have you imprisoned her and punisht her without law and against the Law of god and man... behold my wife without law and against Law is imprison' and punished and so highly condemned for saying the light is the Rule! It is not your light within your rule by which you make and act such lawes for ye have no rule of God's word in the Bible to make a law titled Quakers nor have you any order from the Supreme State of England to make such lawes. Therefore, it must be your light within you is your rule and you walk by... Remember what Jesus Christ said, "If the light that be in you is darkness, how grcat is that darkness."

[illegible] ...conscience, the first and next words after appearance is "You are a Quaker" see the steppes you follow and let their misry be your warning; and then if answer be not made according to the ruling will; away with them to the Cobhole or new Prison, or House of Correction... And now, Gentlemen, consider their ends, and believe it, itt was certaine the Bishop's ruine suddenly followed after their hott pursuance of some godly people by them called Puritans... especially when they proceeded to suck the blood of Mr. Prine, Mr. Burton and Dr. Bostwick's eares, only them three and but three, and they were as odious to them as the Quakers are to you. What witness or legal testimony was taken that my wife Mary Dyre was a Quaker, if not before God and man how can you clear yourselves and seat of justice, from cruelty persecution ye as so fair as in you lies murder as to her and to myself and family oppression and tiranny. The God of trust knows all this. The God of truth knows all this. This is the sum and totals of a law title Quakers: that she is guilty of a breach of a tittled Quakers is as strange, that she is lawfully convicted of two witnesses is not hear of, that she must be banished by law titled Quakers being not convicted by law but considered by surmise and condemned to close prison by Mr. Bellingham's suggestion is so absurd and ridiculous, the meanest pupil in law will hiss at such proceeds in Old Lawyers... is your law titled Quakers Felony or Treason, that vehement suspicion render them capable of suffering... If you be men I suppose your fundamental lawes is that noe person shall be imprisoned or molested but upon the breach of a law, yett behold my wife without law and against law is imprisoned and punished.

My wife writes me word and information, yet she had been above a fortnight and had not trode on the ground, but saw it out your window; what inhumanity is this, had you never wives of your own, or ever any tender affection to a woman, deal so with a woman, what has nature forgotten if refreshment be debarred?

I have written thus plainly to you, being exceedingly sensible of the unjust molestations and detaining of my deare yokefellow, mine and my familyes want of her will crye loud in yo' eares together with her sufferings of your part but I questions not mercy favor and comfort from the most high of her owne soule, that at present my self and family bea by you deprived of the comfort and refreshment we might have enjoyed by her [presence].

Her husband
W. Dyre
Newport this 30 August 1659

Mary Dyer's First Letter from Prison to the General Court

Whereas I am by many charged with the Guiltiness of my own Blood: if you mean in my Coming to Boston, I am therein clear, and justified by the Lord, in whose Will I came, who will require my Blood of you, be sure, who have made a Law to take away the Lives of the Innocent Servants of God, if they come among you who are called by you, 'Cursed Quakers,' altho I say, and am a Living Witness for them and the Lord, that he hath blessed them, and sent them unto you: Therefore, be not found Fighters against God, but let my Counsel and Request be accepted with you, To repeal all such Laws, that the Truth and Servants of the Lord, may have free Passage among you and you be kept from shedding innocent Blood, which I know there are many among you would not do, if they knew it so to be: Nor can the Enemy that stirreth you up thus to destroy this holy Seed, in any Measure contervail, the great Damage that you will by thus doing procure: Therefeore, seeing the Lord hath not hid it from me, it lyeth upon me, in Love to your Souls, thus to persuade you: I have no Self Ends, the Lord knoweth, for if my Life were freely granted by you, it would not avail me, nor could I expect it of you, so long as I shall daily hear and see, of the Sufferings of these People, my dear Brethren and Seed, with whom my Life is bound up, as I have done these two Years, and not it is like to increase, even unto Death for no evil Doing, but Coming among you: Was ever the like laws heard of, among a People that profess Christ come in the Flesh? And have such no other Weapons, but such Laws, to fight with against spiritual Wickedness with all, as you call it? Wo is me for you! Of whom take you Counsel! Search with the light of Christ in you, and it will show you of whom, as it hath done me, and many more, who have been disobedient and deceived, as now you are, which Light, as you come into, and obey what is made manifest to you therein, you will not repent, that you were kept from shedding Blood, tho be a Woman: It's not my own Life I seek (for I chose rather to suffer with the People of God, than to enjoy the Pleasures of Egypt*) but the Life of the Seed, which I know the Lord hath blessed, and therefore seeks the Enemy thus vehemently the Life

*The People of God refers to Jewish slaves while the Pleasures of Egypt refers to the vast wealth of the Egyptian Pharaoh.

thereof to destroy, as in all ages he ever did: Oh! hearken not unto him, I beseech you, for the Seed's Sake, which is One in all, and is dear in the Sight of God; which they that touch, Touch the Apple of his Eye, and cannot escape his Wrath; whereof I having felt, cannot but persuade all men that I have to do withal, especially you who name the Name of Christ, to depart from such Iniquity, as SHEDDING BLOOD, EVEN OF THE SAINTS OF THE MOST HIGHT. Therefore let my Request have as much Acceptance with you, if you be Christians as Esther had with Ahasuerus* whose relation is short of that that's between

Mary Dyer's first letter to the General Court, signed Mary Dyar

*King Ahasuerus is more commonly known as Xerxes (Zerk-ses), a powerful leader of Persia who enslaved the Jews.

78

Christians and my Request is the same that hers was: and he said not, that he had made a Law, and it would be dishonourable for him to revoke it: but when he understood that these People were so prized by her, and so nearly concerned her (as in Truth these are to me) as you may see what he did for her: Therefore I leave these Lines with you, appealing to the faithful and true Witness of God, which is One in all Consciences, before whom we must all appear; with whom I shall eternally rest, in Everlasting Joy and Peace, whether you will hear or forebear: With him is my Reward, with whom to live is my Joy, and to die is my Gain, tho' I had not had your forty-eight Hours Warning, for the Preparation of the Death of Mary Dyar.

And know this also, that if through the Enmity you shall declare yourselves worse than Ahasuerus, and confirm your Law, tho' it were but the taking away the Life of one of us, That the Lord will overthrow both your Law and you, by his righteous Judgments and Plagues poured justly upon you who now whilst you are warned thereof, and tenderly sought unto, may avoid the one, by removing the other; If you neither hear nor obey the Lord nor his Servants, yet will he send more of his Servants among you, so that your End shall be frustrated, that think to restrain them, you call 'Cursed Quakers' from coming among you, by any Thing you can do to them; yea, verily, he hath a Seed here among you, for whom we have suffered all this while, and yet suffer: whom the Lord of the Harvest will send forth more Labourers to gather (out of the Mouths of the Devourers of all sorts) into his Fold, where he will lead them into fresh Pastures, even the Paths of Righteousness, for his Name's Sake: Oh! let none of you put this Day far from you, which verily in the light of the Lord I see approaching, even to many in and about Boston, which is the bitterest and darkest professing Place, and so to continue as long as you have done, that ever I heard of; let the time past therefore suffice, for such a Profession as bring forth such Fruits as these Laws are, In Love and in the Spirit of Meekness, I again beseech you, for I have no Enmity to the Persons of any; but you shall know, that God will not be mocked, but what you sow, that shall you reap from him, that will render to everyone according to the Deeds done in the Body, whether Good or Evil, Even so be it, saith.

Mary Dyar

Mary Dyer's Second Letter from Prison

My life is not accepted, neither availeth me, in Comparison of the Lives and Liberty of the Truth and Servants of the Living God, for which in the Bowels of Love and Meekness I sought you; yet nevertheless, with wicked Hands have you put two of them to Death*, which makes me to feel that the Mercies of the Wicked is Cruelty. I rather chuse to die than to live, as from you, as Guilty of their innocent Blood. Therefore, seeing my Request is hindered, I leave you to the Righteous Judge and Searcher of all Hearts, who, with the pure measure of Light he hath given to every Man to profit withal, will in his due time let you see whose Servants you are, and of whom you have taken Counsel, which desire you to search into: But all his counsel hath been slighted, and you would none of his reproofs. Read your Portion, Proverbs 1:24 to 32. "For verily the Night cometh on you apace, wherein no Man

*The two who have been put to death are Marmaduke Stephenson and William Robinson, seven months before.

can Work, in which you shall assuredly fall to your own Master, in Obedience to the Lord, whom I serve with my Spirit, and to pity to your Souls, which you neither know nor pity: I can do no less than once more to warn you, to put away the Evil of your Doings, and Kiss the Son, the Light in you before his wrath be kindled in you; for where it is, nothing without you can help or deliver you out of his hand at all; and if these things be not so, then say, There hath been no prophet from the Lord sent amongst you: yet it is his Pleasure, by Things that are not, to bring to naught Things that are."

When I heard your last Order read, it was a disturbance unto me, that was so freely Offering up my life to him that give it me, and sent me hither to do, which Obedience being his own Work, he gloriously accompanied with his Presence, and Peace, and Love in me, in which I rested from my labour, till by your Order, and the People, I was so far disturbed that I could not retain anymore of the words thereof than that I should return to Prison, and there remain Forty and Eight hours; to which I submitted, finding nothing from the Lord to the contrary, that I may know what his Pleasure and Counsel is concerning me, on whom I wait therefore, for he is my Life, and the length of my Days, and as

I said before, I came at his command, and go at His command.

Mary Dyar
May 31, 1660

William Dyer's Letter to the General Court

Honor S[irs],

It is not little greif of mind and sadness of hart that I am necessitated to be so bold as to supplicate you' Honor self w' the Honorable Assembly of yo' Generall Courte to extend yo' mercy and favo' once agen to me and my children, little did I dream that I shuld have had occasion to petition you in a matter of this nature, but so it is that [through] the devine **providence** and yo' benignity my sonn obtayned so much pitty and meicy att yo' hands as to enjoy the life of his mother, now my supplication yo' Hono' is to begg affectionately, the life of my deare wife, tis true I have not seen her about this half yeare and therefor cannot tell how in the frame of her spiritt

83

she was moved thus againe to runn so great a Hazard to herself, and perplexity to me and mine and all her friends and well wishers; so itt is from Shelter Island about by Pequid Narragansett and to the Towne of Providence she secrettly and speedyly journyed, and as secretly from thence came to yo' jurisdiction, unhappy journy may I say, and woe to thee at generatcon [*General Court?—editor*] say I that gives occasion thus of grief and troble (to those that desire to be quiett) by helping one another (as I may say) to Hazard their lives for I know not watt end or to what purpose; If her zeale be so greatt as thus to adventure, oh lett your favoure and pitty surmount itt and save her life. Let not yo' forwanted Compassion bee conquared by her inconsiderate maddnesse, and how greatly will yo' renowne be spread if by so conquering yo' become victorious, what shall I say more, I know yo'are all sensible of my condition, and lett the reflect bee, and you will see whatt my [petition] is and what will give me and mine peace, oh Lett mercies wings once more sore above justice ballance, and then whilst I live shall I exalt yo' goodness butt other wayes twill be a languishing sorrow, yea so great that I shuld gladly suffer this blow att once much rather: I shall forebear to troble yo' Hn' with words neyther am I in capacity to expatiate myself at present; I only say that yo'selves have been and are or may bee husbands to wife or wives, so am I: yea to once most dearely beloved: oh do not you deprive me of her, but I pray give her me once agen and I shall bee so much obleiged for ever that I shall endeavor continually to utter my thanks and render you Love and Honor most renowned: pitty me, I begg itt with teares, and rest you.

Most humbly suppliant
W. Dyre
Portsmouth 27 of [May] 1660

TIMELINE

1607	Jamestown founded in Virginia.
1609	William Dyer is born. The bubonic plague devastates London.
1611?	Mary Dyer is born.
1616	William Shakespeare dies.
1619	First African slaves arrive in North America.
1620	Pilgrims land at Plymouth Rock.

1625	James I dies. Charles I crowned.
1630	Boston, Massachusetts founded.
1633	William Dyer weds Mary Barrett.
1634-1638	Pequot War fought.
1635	The Dyers move to Boston.
1636	Roger Williams founds Rhode Island.
1638	Antinomians banned from Boston. Portsmouth Compact signed.
1642-1651	English Civil War fought.
1643	Anne Hutchinson murdered.
1652-1654	First Anglo-Dutch War fought.
1657	Mary Dyer arrested for being a Quaker.
1658	Oliver Cromwell dies.

1659	First two Boston Martyrs hanged.
1660 May	Charles II crowned.
1660 June	Mary Dyer hanged for her beliefs.
1661	Last of the Boston Martyrs hanged.
1677	William Dyer dies.
1681	Pennsylvania founded by William Penn.
1685	Charles II dies. James II crowned.
1689	Toleration Acts passed.
1775-1783	The Revolutionary War fought. America gains its independence.
1777	Thomas Jefferson writes the Virginia Statute for Religious Freedom.
1786	The Virginia Statute for Religious Freedom becomes law.

1791	The U.S. Constitution guarantees religious freedom for everyone following the passage of the First Amendment.
1959	Massachusetts erects a statue of Mary Dyer at the State House.
1996	The Anne Hutchinson/Mary Dyer Herb Garden created at Founders' Brook Park in Portsmouth, Rhode Island.
1998	October 27th declared International Religious Freedom Day.

HISTORICAL FIGURES

The Antinomians: A group of Boston citizens led by Anne Hutchinson that hoped to change the beliefs of the Puritan Church. Their name means "against the law."

The Boston Martyrs: Four people—Marmaduke Stephenson, William Robinson, Mary Dyer, and William Leddra—executed between 1659-1661 for being Quakers.

Anne Bradstreet (1612-1672): America's first published poet.

Canonicus (1565-1647): A powerful Narragansett sachem who was Miantonomoh's uncle.

Charles I (1600-1649): Protestant king of England who eased religious restrictions after marrying a Catholic. Executed by the Roundheads during the English Civil War.

Charles II (1639-1685): Protestant king of England who enforced religious protections following Mary Dyer's death.

William Coddington (1601-1678): An early supporter of Anne Hutchinson and a founder of Portsmouth, Rhode Island.

Oliver Cromwell (1599-1658): Puritan leader of the Roundheads and victor in the English Civil War.

John Cotton (1585-1652): Puritan minister in Boston.

John Endecott (1601-1664/5): Governor and military leader of Boston who sentenced Mary Dyer to die.

George Fox (1624-1691): Founder of the Quakers, formally known as the Religious Society of Friends.

Anne Hutchinson (1591-1643): Leader of the Antinomians and strong advocate for religious tolerance and women's rights.

James I (1566-1625): Protestant king of England who persecuted Catholics and witches, and wrote the most famous translation of the Bible.

James II (1633-1701): Catholic king of England who enforced religious protections following Mary Dyer's death. Son of Charles I and brother of Charles II.

Miantonomoh (1600-1643): A powerful Narragansett sachem who was friendly to the English colonists.

William Penn (1644-1718): A Quaker who founded the state of Pennsylvania and the city of Philadelphia.

The Puritans: A religious group that wished to "purify" the religious teachings of the Anglican Church.

Henry Vane (1613-1662): A one-term governor of the Massachusetts Bay Colony who protected Anne Hutchinson from being charged with religious crimes.

Giovanni da Verrazano (1485-1528): An Italian explorer who sailed for France and provided early descriptions of the Narragansett.

Roger Williams (1603-1683): A Puritan minister who founded Rhode Island and the city of Providence, as well as the first Baptist church in North America.

John Wilson (1591-1667): A minister who banished Anne Hutchinson from the Puritan Church and oversaw the death of Mary Dyer.

John Winthrop (1587-1649): The governor of Massachusetts Bay Colony who banished Anne Hutchinson, William Dyer and other Antinomians from Boston. His son later banished Mary from preaching in New Haven, Connecticut.

GLOSSARY

Abolitionist: A person who wishes to abolish, or end, slavery.

Amendment: A change or addition to a law.

Bill of Rights: The first ten amendments to the U.S. Constitution guaranteeing certain freedoms for all citizens.

Constitution: The set of laws that govern a country.

Heresy: The act of defying or disbelieving a certain religious belief.

Martyr: A person who dies for a cause they believe in.

Pacifist: A person who does not believe in fighting a war for any reason.

Parchment: Paper made from sheep or goat skin and often used for important documents.

Petition: The act of asking the government to change certain laws or actions.

Providence: Receiving divine care and guidance.

Tyranny: Cruel and abusive power, or a system of government in which one person (a tyrant) uses such power.

PAINTINGS

Page 5: Lady Arabella Stuart by Robert Peake the Elder, Scottish National Portrait Gallery

Page 5: William, Marq. Of Hertford (likely) by Gilbert Jackson

Page 11: Based on George Lamb's Plan of Boston Showing Existing Ways and Owncrs, December 25, 1635

Page 14: Roger Williams and the Narragansett by James Charles Armytage, 1856, New York Public Library

Page 15: Anne Hutchinson on Trial by Edwin Austin Abbey, 1901, Harvard College Library

Page 20: Anne Bradstreet at Work, 19th-century painting

Page 25: Uncas executes Miantonomoh by Edmund Ollier, *Cassell's History of the United States*

Page 35: A Huron longhouse by Donnacona, 2006

Page 37: Massacre of Anne Hutchinson, 1878, *A Popular History of the United States*

Page 42: Battle of the Gabbard, 2 June 1653 by Heerman Witmont, National Maritime Museum

Page 44: Portrait of George Fox (likely) by Peter Lely, Swarthmore College

Page 91: Portrait of John Cotton, 1856, *History of Boston Antiquities*

Page 92: Portrait of James II in Garter Robes by Peter Lely, 1689

Page 93: William Penn, 1718

Page 93: Giovanni da Verrazzano, Galleria Comunale

Page 94: Portrait of John Wilson by A.B. Ellis, 1881, *History of the First Church in Boston,* 1630-1880

Find color images of many of these paintings at *johnbriggsbooks.net!*

RESOURCE MATERIALS

Books

James, Edward T. *Notable American Women: A Biographical Dictionary*, Radcliffe College, 1971

Jarvis, Brian. *Mary Dyer, The Play: She Died Twice Oxford Dictionary of National Biography*

Plimpton, Ruth Talbot. *Mary Dyer: Biography of a Rebel Quaker*, Branden Publishing Co., 1994

Roberts, Gary Boyd. *Genealogies of Rhode Island Families, Volume I Alden-Mowry*, Genealogical Publishing Company, Inc., 1989

Rogers, Horatio. *Mary Dyer of Rhode Island: The Quaker Martyr That Was Hanged On Boston Common, June 1, 1660*, Ulan Press, 2012

Willis, Garry. *Head and Heart: American Christianities, "Mary Dyer Must Die,"* Penguin, 2007

Websites

Ancestry.com, *Mary Barrett Dyer*

DyerFarm.com, *Mary Dyer: Quaker Martyr and Enigma*, 2008

Gale Cengage Learning, *Mary Dyer Trials: 1659 and 1660*

Gier, Nick. *The Persecution of Quakers,* University of Idaho

LynnGallup.org/Appendix—*Mary Barrett Dyer: Winfield's Martyred Great... Great Grandmother*

MaryBarrettDyer.blogspot, *William and Mary Barrett Dyer*

MaryBarrettDyer.blogspot, W*illiam Dyer: Landlord, Gentleman*

Smitty's Genealogy, Quaker and Civil War Pages, *Martyrdom of Mary Dyer*

United States Geological Survey, *Earthquakes/Events 1638*

Additional Sources

New World Encyclopedia – Anne Hutchinson

New World Encyclopedia – Roger Williams

ReligiousTolerance.org

Salemwitchtrials.com

UPCOMING BOOKS FROM

ATOMBANK'S

BIG BIOGRAPHY SERIES

JUDY GARLAND: LITTLE WOMAN, BIG TALENT

PETE SEEGER, THE PEOPLE'S SINGER

JIM THORPE, ATHLETE OF THE CENTURY

LOOK FOR THEM SOON AT

ATOMBANKBOOKS.COM!

Made in the USA
San Bernardino, CA
01 January 2020

62545563R00062